■SCHOLASTIC

READ &  RESPOND

Helping children discover the pleasure and po[w]

T0333717

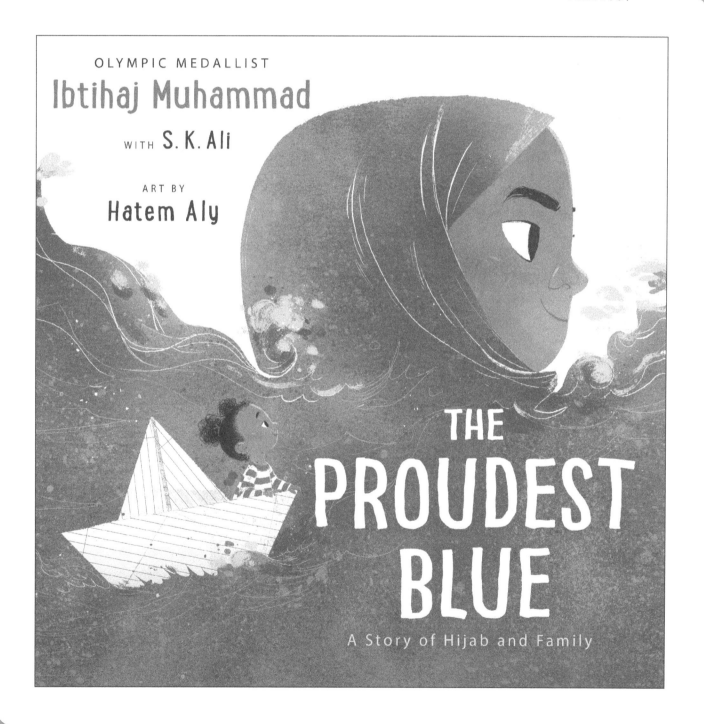

OLYMPIC MEDALLIST
Ibtihaj Muhammad
WITH **S. K. Ali**

ART BY
Hatem Aly

THE PROUDEST BLUE

A Story of Hijab and Family

FOR AGES 5–7

Published in the UK by Scholastic Education, 2022
Scholastic Distribution Centre, Bosworth Avenue, Tournament Fields, Warwick, CV34 6UQ
Scholastic Ireland, 89E Lagan Road, Dublin Industrial Estate, Glasnevin, Dublin, D11 HP5F

1 2 3 4 5 6 7 8 9   2 3 4 5 6 7 8 9 0 1
Printed and bound by Ashford Colour Press

This book is made of materials from well-managed,
FSC®-certified forests and other controlled sources.

A CIP catalogue record for this book is available from the British Library.
ISBN 978-0702-31945-7

Due to the nature of the web, we cannot guarantee the content or links of any site mentioned. We strongly recommend that teachers check websites before using them in the classroom.

Author Charlotte King
Editorial team Rachel Morgan, Vicki Yates, Suzanne Adams, Julia Roberts
Series designer Andrea Lewis
Typesetter QBS Learning
Illustrator Borghild Marie Fullberg

Acknowledgements
The publishers gratefully acknowledge permission to reproduce the following copyright material:
Anderson Press Ltd for the use of the text extracts and cover from *The Proudest Blue* by Ibtihaj Muhammad with SK Ali. Text © 2020.

Every effort has been made to trace copyright holders for the works reproduced in this book, and the publishers apologise for any inadvertent omissions.

For supporting online resources go to:
www.scholastic.co.uk/read-and-respond/books/the-proudest-blue/online-resources
Access key: Once

CONTENTS ▽

How to use Read & Respond in your classroom...

Read & Respond provides teaching ideas related to a specific well-loved children's book. Each Read & Respond book is divided into the following sections:

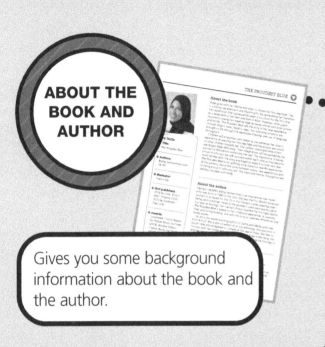

ABOUT THE BOOK AND AUTHOR

Gives you some background information about the book and the author.

GUIDED READING

Breaks the book down into sections and gives notes for using it, ideal for use with the whole class. A bookmark has been provided on page 10 containing **comprehension** questions. The children can be directed to refer to these as they read. Find comprehensive guided reading sessions on the supporting online resources.

SHARED READING

Provides extracts from the children's book with associated notes for focused work. There is also one non-fiction extract that relates to the children's book.

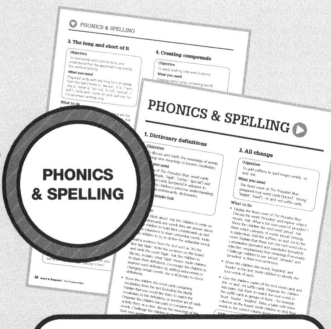

PHONICS & SPELLING

Provides word-level work related to the children's book so you can teach phonics, spelling and **vocabulary** in context.

PLOT, CHARACTER & SETTING

Contains activity ideas focused on the plot, characters and the setting of the story.

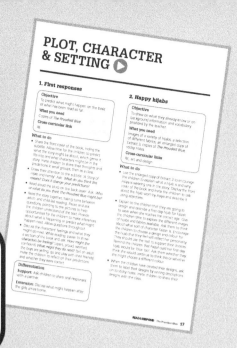

TALK ABOUT IT

Oracy, **fluency**, and speaking and listening activities. These activities may be based directly on the children's book or be broadly based on the themes and concepts of the story.

GET WRITING

Provides writing activities related to the children's book. These activities may be based directly on the children's book or be broadly based on the themes and concepts of the story.

ASSESSMENT

Contains short activities that will help you assess whether the children have understood concepts and curriculum objectives. They are designed to be informal activities to feed into your planning.

SUPPORTING ONLINE RESOURCE

Online you can find a host of supporting documents including planning information, comprehensive guided reading sessions and guidance on teaching reading.

www.scholastic.co.uk/read-and-respond/books/the-proudest-blue/online-resources

Access key: Once

Help children develop a love of reading for pleasure.

Activities

The activities follow the same format:

- **Objective:** the objective for the lesson. It will be based upon a curriculum objective, but will often be more specific to the focus being covered.

- **What you need:** a list of resources you need to teach the lesson, including photocopiable pages.

- **What to do:** the activity notes.

- **Differentiation:** this is provided where specific and useful differentiation advice can be given to support and/or extend the learning in the activity. Differentiation by providing additional adult support has not been included as this will be at a teacher's discretion based upon specific children's needs and ability, as well as the availability of support.

The activities are numbered for reference within each section and should move through the text sequentially – so you can use the lesson while you are reading the book. Once you have read the book, most of the activities can be used in any order you wish.

Section	Activity	Curriculum objectives
Guided reading		Comprehension: To participate in discussion about books that are read to them, taking turns and listening to what others say. To explain and discuss their understanding of books.
Shared reading	1	Spoken language: To maintain attention and participate actively in collaborative conversations, staying on topic and initiating and responding to comments.
	2	Spoken language: To articulate and justify answers, arguments and opinions.
	3	Spoken language: To use relevant strategies to build their vocabulary.
Phonics & spelling	1	Comprehension: To discuss and clarify the meanings of words, linking new meanings to known vocabulary.
	2	Spelling: To add suffixes to spell longer words: -er and -est.
	3	Word reading: To read words with contractions, and understand that the apostrophe represents the omitted letter(s).
	4	Transcription: To apply spelling rules and guidance.
Plot, character & setting	1	Comprehension: To predict what might happen on the basis of what has been read so far.
	2	Comprehension: To draw on what they already know or on background information and vocabulary provided by the teacher.
	3	Comprehension: To discuss the sequence of events in books and how items of information are related.
	4	Comprehension: To draw on what they already know or on background information and vocabulary provided by the teacher.
	5	Comprehension: To discuss word meanings, linking new meanings to those already known.
	6	Comprehension: To draw on what they already know or on background information and vocabulary provided by the teacher.
Talk about it	1	Spoken language: To articulate and justify answers, arguments and opinions.
	2	Spoken language: To participate in role play and improvisations.
	3	Spoken language: To select and use appropriate registers for effective communication.
	4	Spoken language: To participate in discussions and debates.
	5	Spoken language: To give well-structured descriptions, explanations and narratives for different purposes, including for expressing feelings.
	6	Spoken language: To articulate and justify answers, arguments and opinions.
Get writing	1	Handwriting: To write capital letters and digits of the correct size, orientation and relationship to one another and to lower-case letters.
	2	Vocabulary, grammar and punctuation: To use expanded noun phrases to describe and specify.
	3	Composition: To develop positive attitudes towards and stamina for writing by writing for different purposes.
	4	Composition: To plan or say out loud what they are going to write about.
	5	Composition: To write for different purposes.
	6	Composition: To write narratives about personal experiences and those of others.
Assessment	1	Transcription: To write from memory simple sentences dictated by the teacher that include words using the GPCs, common exception words and punctuation taught so far.
	2	Comprehension: To answer and ask questions.
	3	Transcription: To learn to spell more words with contracted forms.
	4	Vocabulary, grammar and punctuation: To use sentences with different forms: statement, question, exclamation, command.

Key facts

◉ **Title:**
The Proudest Blue

◉ **Authors:**
Ibtihaj Muhammad with
SK Ali

◉ **Illustrator:**
Hatem Aly

◉ **First published:**
2019 by Little, Brown
and Company (USA)
2020 by Andersen
Press (UK)

◉ **Awards:**
Goodreads Choice Award
for Picture Books nominee
(2019), Booklist Editors'
Choice: Books for Youth
(2019), Rise: A Feminist
Book Project top ten
(2020), ALSC's Notable
Children's Books (2020)

◉ **Did you know?**
Ibtihaj Muhammad's
mother suggested fencing
as the sport for her so that
she could dress modestly
with long sleeves and
covered legs.

About the book

Asiya goes with her Mama and sister to choose her first-day hijab. This is a pivotal experience in any Muslim girl's life, symbolising her transition into adulthood. She subsequently wears it to school for the first time as a testament to her faith and love of Allah. However, other pupils respond to seeing her wearing hijab by being unkind with both actions and words. *The Proudest Blue* tells the story of this new experience through Asiya's sister, Faizah's, eyes. Her confusing emotions are brought to life through the expressive drawings and use of language throughout.

Children will empathise with Faizah as she witnesses her sister's experience of wearing her first-day hijab and the actions and words of other children towards her. She cannot understand why others see Asiya's hijab differently. Their imaginations will be sparked by the wonderful illustrations enhancing the text. The importance of being proud of who you are will resonate within each child as they become more familiar with the story and begin to relate it to their own lives. *The Proudest Blue* is an uplifting story, based on real-life experiences of the authors, about the bond between sisters, new experiences and of being proud of who you are. The important themes throughout are identity, courage and family.

About the author

Olympic medallist Ibtihaj Muhammad is an inspirational role model who was born in 1985 in the USA. She was the first Muslim American woman to compete for the US in the Olympic Games wearing hijab. Ibtihaj won a bronze medal in the women's sabre team events (sabre is a type of fencing). Her memoir, *Proud*, inspired the first hijabi Barbie. *The Proudest Blue* is based on her childhood experiences of wearing hijab and facing bullying. She tells the story to celebrate differences and family values.

SK Ali is the award-winning author of *Saints and Misfits* and *Love from A to Z*. She is also co-editor of an Eid anthology. She was born in South India and emigrated to Canada at the age of three. She lives in Toronto with her family and cat. Like Faizah and Asiya in the story, she and her sister used to visit hijab shops every year, before the first day of school, to choose their proudest colours.

About the illustrator

Hatem Aly, born in Egypt, has illustrated many books. His pictures for *The Proudest Blue* were influenced by his childhood memories of playing with his mum's colourful scarves and sharing his opinion on which she should wear. Hatem lives in Canada with his wife, son and many pets.

GUIDED READING ▶

Introducing the book

Hold up the front cover of the book and explore the illustration together. Allow the children time to focus on the picture and to share their thoughts with a partner. Invite children to share with the class their predictions around any content that may be in the story. Read the title and ask the children questions 1 and 2 on the bookmark. Establish that the book is 'A Story of Hijab and Family'. Ask: *What do you think a hijab might be?* (a boat, travel, the sea, a scarf) Refer back to the illustration and search for clues about the meaning of the word 'hijab'. (a head covering worn in public by some Muslim women) While exploring the illustration, invite children to predict how the two people are related. Remind them that the story is about family. Identify any possible clues from the illustration about where the story might take place.

Draw attention to the names Ibtihaj Muhammad, SK Ali and Hatem Aly and ask if the children have heard of any of them. Establish which ones are the authors and which one is the illustrator. (Refer to page 7 for more information about them all.) Ensure that the children know that the story is based on the real-life experiences of the authors.

Turn to the back cover and discuss the illustration with the children. Read the blurb and challenge them to identify who they think is the main character (Asiya or her sister)? Ask: *What do we now know about the main characters?* (One of them is called Asiya and she has a sister.) Once the children have had time to finish exploring the cover, ask them to voice their first impressions of the book.

Initial reading of the book

Divide your initial reading of the story into four sections. This will allow time to focus on the different aspects of the text and compare and contrast emotions, events and characters within the story. When reading aloud, ensure your reading sparks the children's imaginations, allowing them to vividly imagine each event and helping them to build a picture in their minds of the characters and emotions they are feeling.

In order to develop children's spoken language, ensure that the children hear language which is clear, varied and of a high quality. Taking part in guided reading activities should help to develop pupils' confidence and competence in spoken language and listening skills.

Section 1 (first three double-page spreads)

As you read this first section, focus on helping the children to understand the meaning of the text through appropriate comments and questions. Ask questions from the bookmark to establish what is meant by certain phrases and vocabulary.

Focus on the first double-page spread of the story and discuss how it sets the scene for the book. Ask: *Where is the action taking place?* If children find this question difficult, look back at the illustrations preceding the title page and the beginning of the story. (There is a double-page spread featuring a shop with a sign reading 'Hijabs' and a picture of the inside of the shop with the shopkeeper.)

Draw the children's attention to the language used to describe the material behind the counter. Discuss why effective description is so important in helping to establish 'mind's eye' images. Comment together on how the description conjures up images of the ocean and the horizon. Encourage the children to identify the scarf that the words are describing.

Ask the children question 8 on the bookmark and encourage them to find some examples in the text. Discuss what this tells the reader about Faizah's character. (She is excited, happy, carefree.) Refer to the sentence 'I'm walking with a princess.' Ask: *What does this tell us about Faizah's opinion of her older sister?* (She admires her. She thinks she's important.) Invite children to find words that show the story is written from Faizah's point of view ('I', 'we're', 'I'm', 'my', 'me') and discuss the first-person narrative. Draw attention to this as you continue to read the story.

When reading the final double-page spread in this section, ask the children to start thinking about question 7 on the bookmark. Invite them to identify a phrase on the page which personifies the hijab. ('Her hijab smiles at me the whole way.')

Section 2 (next three double-page spreads)

Before reading this section, ask: *Can you predict what will happen once Asiya walks away?* Remind the children that it is the first time she is wearing hijab. Draw their attention to the other people in the picture. Ask: *Is anyone else wearing hijab?*

Read through the pages with appropriate intonation and expression. Draw the children's attention to the rich illustrations and compare the use of colours in each double-page spread. Focus on the facial expressions of the children and discuss how each one is feeling. Pay particular attention to Asiya's expression and compare it to Faizah's. Encourage the children to take part in echo reading during this section, applying different dynamics to their reading.

Ask the children question 5 on the bookmark and discuss their opinions. Explain that the words in italics are Mama's words of advice to Asiya.

Section 3 (next six double-page spreads)

As you read through this section together, invite the children to consider how Faizah's and Asiya's feelings have changed as the story has progressed – from excitement when choosing the hijab to apprehension entering the school playground, to feeling proud and joyful, to feeling angry and upset towards the other children. Encourage the children to make comparisons with similar emotional experiences of their own and to share these experiences with the class. The focus of the discussion will be swayed by the children's own comments and ideas.

Draw the children's attention to the illustrations, especially the unkind boys illustrated as shadowy figures without facial features, and the use of colour when comparing the feelings of the different characters. Pose question 6 on the bookmark. Encourage the children to voice their opinions and discuss why the artist portrayed the yelling boy like that.

Section 4 (next three double-page spreads)

When reading this final section, talk with the children about the emotions experienced by the characters so far in the story. Pose question 3 on the bookmark. Allow time for the children to debate whether they think Faizah or Asiya is the main character and why. (Faizah, because she is telling the story; Asiya, as the book is all about her wearing hijab for the first time.)

Show the children the three double-page spreads that make up this section and ask question 4 on the bookmark. At this point, you may need to display images and read sections of text from earlier in the story to remind the children about the different settings, for example, the girls in the shop with their Mama, the girls in the playground, Faizah in class, the girls walking home.

As the story draws to a close, ask question 10 on the bookmark. Discuss the children's replies and establish their understanding of the importance of the bond between the sisters in the story. Talk about how Faizah cares and worries about Asiya, and how Asiya takes care of Faizah. Invite the children to find examples in this final section to support this. Ask question 9 on the bookmark. Encourage the children to link their own experiences to those of the characters. Ask: *Which character might have felt proud and why?* (Faizah, because her sister is not affected by the yelling boys.)

After reading

After exploring the settings, characters and events in the story, encourage the children to reconsider their initial thoughts on and impressions of the book. Allow the children to ask any questions they have about the book or to query anything they are uncertain about. Remind the children to refer back to the text in order to support their questions and answers. Having considered their thoughts and impressions, this could be an ideal time to invite the children to write a book review.

The Proudest Blue
by Ibtihaj Muhammad with SK Ali

Focus on... Meaning

1. What do you think the story might be about? Does the title help you to answer the question?

2. Who or what do you think *The Proudest Blue* might be? What makes you think this?

3. Do you think there is one main character in the story, or more than one? Why do you think this?

Focus on... Organisation

4. Name the different settings in the story. What clues do the illustrations and text provide to help you with your answer?

5. Find some words written in italics. What do you think is the author's reason for doing this?

The Proudest Blue
by Ibtihaj Muhammad with SK Ali

Focus on... Language and features

6. What do you think about Hatem Aly's illustrations? What effect do they have on the reader as they read the story?

7. How does the author bring the hijab to life? Can you find examples in the text?

8. Focus on the language used to show how Faizah moves. What does this tell you about her character?

Focus on... Purpose, viewpoints and effects

9. Have you ever felt proud? Can you describe the feeling? What did you do to make yourself feel proud?

10. What do you think the story tells us about the bond between the sisters in the story? Find a section of the text to support your answer.

SHARED READING ▶

Extract 1

- Display and read an enlarged copy of Extract 1. Explain that this is the opening section of the story. Invite children to identify the setting (a shop selling hijabs) and the name of the main character. (The reader does not find out Faizah's name until later.) Underline the first two sentences. Invite children to say what is different about the way they are written (all in capitals). Ask: *Why do you think the author decided to write them in that way?* (They are important. Mama's opinion matters to the narrator.) Encourage the children to suggest possible plot events from the clues in the text (first-day hijab).

- Highlight any words that are less familiar to the children such as 'squint', 'pretend', 'hijab'. Invite children to share their ideas regarding the definitions of the words. Underline the contractions 'there's', 'It's', 'We're'. Re-read the sentences without the contractions and discuss whether the rhythm sounds the same. Ask: *Which do you think are most effective?*

- Discuss whether or not this extract makes a good beginning, encouraging the children to give reasons for their decision.

Extract 2

- Introduce Extract 2 by explaining that it is an event from the middle of the book. Display and read together an enlarged copy of the extract.

- Re-read the sentence 'They race to the middle of the playground, their shoes pounding the pavement, playing tag.' Highlight all the words beginning with 'p'. Ask: *What effect does the repetition of the 'p' initial sound have on the sentence?'* Establish that alliteration strengthens the rhythm of the sentence. Invite children to read the sentence expressively. Compare this sentence to the two sentences preceding it. Challenge the children to suggest ways in which they could be read differently to mirror the altering emotions.

- Highlight Mama's advice. Discuss the way it is written (in italics). Ask: *Why do you think it is written in italics rather than as direct speech?* (It makes the words stand out. The reader can find it easily.) Invite children to take turns reading the advice expressively. Underline 'carry', 'Drop' and 'keep'. Ask: *Can you carry, drop and keep words? What do you think the author means?* Encourage the children to make links between the advice given and Asiya running away.

Extract 3

- Display an enlarged copy of Extract 3, with only the heading showing. Ask: *Do you think this page is fiction or non-fiction?* Encourage the children to give reasons for their answers. Highlight the word 'facts' and discuss its meaning.

- Reveal the whole page and establish that the words in bold are repeated in the box at the bottom of the page. Divide the class into eight small groups and ask them to read aloud one fact each. Ask the rest of the class to support them with reading the words in bold.

- Return to the bold words and ensure, by discussion and explanation, that the children understand the meaning of each one. The children could use dictionaries to help them with this activity. When all the bold words have been discussed, cover the facts and challenge the children to recall the meaning of the words.

Extract 1

MAMA HOLDS OUT THE PINK.
MAMA LOVES PINK.
But Asiya shakes her head.
I know why.

Behind the counter is the brightest blue.
The colour of the ocean,
if you squint your eyes and
pretend there's no line
between the water
and the sky.

It's the first-day hijab.
Asiya knows it. I know it.
We're sisters.

Extract 2

Asiya turns away. Her friends turn away.

They race to the middle of the playground, their shoes pounding the pavement, playing tag.

Mama: *Don't carry around the hurtful words that others say. Drop them. They are not yours to keep.*

They belong only to those who said them.

Extract 3
Ten fantastic facts

Islam is the name of the religion that a **Muslim** person follows.

Muslims believe in one God, named **Allah**, who created everything.

Muhammad was the last **prophet**.

The religious book of Islam is called the **Qur'an**.

In Islam, most females start wearing **hijab** from about age 10 to 14 to show they are now adults.

The word hijab is used to refer to clothing which covers a woman's chest, head and hair.

A woman wears a hijab when she is with a man that is not in her immediate family.

There is a wide variety of hijab styles. Some are dark, others are bright. Some are plain while others have patterns or embroidery.

Interesting vocabulary

Islam   Muslim   Allah   Muhammad   prophet   Qur'an   hijab

PHONICS & SPELLING ▶

1. Dictionary definitions

Objective
To discuss and clarify the meanings of words, linking new meanings to known vocabulary.

What you need
Copies of *The Proudest Blue*, word cards (for example, 'hijab', 'curtsy', 'special') and definition cards (prepared in advance to reflect the children's previous understanding), individual whiteboards, dictionaries.

Cross-curricular link
RE

What to do
- Read the blurb aloud. Ask the children to write on their whiteboards any words they are unsure about. Tell the children to hold their whiteboards up and ask for volunteers to share unfamiliar words. Invite other children to try to define the unfamiliar words.

- Read a sentence from the text such as 'It's the first-day hijab.' Write the sentence on the board and circle the word 'hijab'. Ask the children to discuss, in pairs, what 'hijab' means. Invite children to share their definitions. Encourage the children to improve each definition by adding extra words or changing certain words. Use a dictionary to check definitions.

- Show the children the word cards containing vocabulary from the text (including the blurb). Explain that you would like them to match the vocabulary to the definitions on another set of cards. Organise the children into pairs to complete the activity then, as a class, discuss the meanings of the words. Challenge the children to use the words in their own sentences.

Differentiation
Support: Allow children to focus on lower-level vocabulary to match to definitions.

Extension: Encourage children to write their own definitions prior to identifying matching pairs.

2. All change

Objective
To add suffixes to spell longer words: -er and -est.

What you need
The front cover of *The Proudest Blue*, prepared root word cards ('proud', 'strong', 'bright', 'loud'), -er and -est suffix cards.

What to do
- Display the front cover of *The Proudest Blue*. Discuss the word 'Proudest' and explore what it means. Ask: *What is the root word of* 'proudest'? Show the children the root word 'proud'. Ask them which category of words 'proud' belongs to (adjective). Add the suffixes -er and -est to the word. Explain that these turn the root word into a comparative (prouder) and superlative (proudest) adjective, emphasising their meanings if necessary. Challenge children to use 'proud', 'prouder' and 'proudest' in their own sentences.

- Show the children the words 'brightest' and 'louder' in the text. Invite children to identify the root words of each.

- Give the children copies of the root word cards and the -er and -est suffix cards. Organise the children into pairs. Ask them to match the root words to the suffix cards in groups of three – for example, 'loud', 'louder', 'loudest'. Draw a table with three columns on the board. Invite children to stick their words in the correct column (root word, -er, -est).

Differentiation
Support: Ensure the words are at an appropriate phonic level for children to read.

Extension: Give children exception cards among their choices, including words such as 'happy' and 'good'. Invite children to explore and discuss the rule for adding suffixes.

3. The long and short of it

Objective
To read words with contractions, and understand that the apostrophe represents the omitted letter(s).

What you need
Prepared cards with the long form of words from the text ('there is', 'we are', 'it is', 'I am', 'she is', 'what is', 'do not', 'is not', 'cannot', 'I will'). Cards with 'come on' and 'will not' for the extension activity only.

What to do
- Write an apostrophe on the board and ask the children to discuss what it is with a partner. Ask volunteers to share their answers and challenge them to give examples by using a word containing an apostrophe in a sentence. Explain that they will be making contracted forms of words using apostrophes. Define the meaning of 'contracted' if necessary.

- Show the children the long form card for 'there is'. Model using 'there is' in a sentence, for example, 'There is a blue hijab in the story.' Model cutting the card either side of the 'i', sticking 'there' on a sheet of paper, adding an apostrophe, then sticking 's' after it. Choose a child to read the contracted form of the word ('there's'). Ask: *Can you change the original sentence using the contracted form?* ('There's a blue hijab in the story.')

- Let the children use the long form of words cards, cutting and sticking them to create contracted forms using apostrophes. Bring the children together and ask them to share their contracted forms with each other. Invite children to use them in sentences.

- Show them the words 'sister's', 'Asiya's' and 'kids'. Discuss with the children why these words are different. Ask: *What is the purpose of the apostrophe in these words?*

Differentiation
Support: Give children words within their phonic knowledge such as 'it is' and 'I am'.

Extension: Include the cards 'will not' and 'come on' from the text. Discuss 'c'mon'.

4. Creating compounds

Objective
To apply spelling rules and guidance.

What you need
Prepared word cards containing words that can be used to create compound words (back/pack, cart/wheel, play/ground, good/bye, some/one, under/stand, table/cloth, speed-walk, light-up, first-day), individual whiteboards.

What to do
- Revise how to split words into syllables. Write on the board three words from *The Proudest Blue* with one, two and three syllables (for example, 'cross', 'princess', 'beautiful'), and ask the children to identify which is which by clapping the syllables.

- Explain that some words can be separated into two separate words (table/cloth). Discuss the meaning of the two separate words and the compound word made by them.

- Display six words on the board that can be used to create compound words. Invite the children to decide on a new word that can be created by combining a pair of words. Encourage them to use any new words orally in sentences. Explain that some compound words can be hyphenated ('speed-walk', 'light-up'). Remind the children that each part of the compound word is spelt as it would be if it were on its own.

- Give out the word cards for the children to use to create compound words from the text. Once they have matched the pairs, ask them to write the compound words. Share the results as a class, counting the syllables in each word. Challenge the children to use their compound words in a sentence. Invite them to clap the syllables as they orally dictate their sentence for a partner to write down. Ask the children to check and correct, if necessary, the spelling of the compound word.

Differentiation
Support: Limit pairs of words so there are fewer choices, or colour-code the cards so that children can create compound words by matching colours.

Extension: Challenge children to find as many compound words in the text as they can.

PLOT, CHARACTER & SETTING ▶

1. First responses

Objective
To predict what might happen on the basis of what has been read so far.

What you need
Copies of *The Proudest Blue*.

Cross-curricular link
RE

What to do

- Share the front cover of the book, hiding the subtitle. Allow time for the children to predict what the story might be about, which genre it fits into and what characters might be in the story. Invite children to share their thoughts and predictions in small groups, then as a class.

- Draw their attention to the subtitle: 'A Story of Hijab and Family'. Ask: *What do you think this means? Does it change your predictions?*

- Read aloud the blurb on the back cover. Ask: *Who or what do you think The Proudest Blue might be?*

- Read the story together, taking turns between adult- and child-led reading. Pause and ask questions, pointing to the pictures to help the children understand of the text. Provide opportunities for the children to make inferences about what is happening or predict what might happen next. Allow questions throughout.

- Discuss the characters' feelings and what they might do next. While reading, pause to show a section of the book and ask: *How might the characters be feeling?* (upset, proud, worried, confident) *What might they do next?* (tell an adult the boys are yelling; go and play with their friends) Invite the children to reflect on their predictions and whether they were correct.

Differentiation

Support: Ask children to share oral responses with a partner.

Extension: Discuss what might happen after the girls arrive home.

2. Happy hijabs

Objective
To draw on what they already know or on background information and vocabulary provided by the teacher.

What you need
Images of a variety of hijabs, a selection of different fabrics, an enlarged copy of Extract 3, copies of *The Proudest Blue*, sticky notes.

Cross-curricular links
RE, art and design

What to do

- Use the enlarged copy of Extract 3 to encourage the children to explain what a hijab is and why Asiya is wearing one in the story. Display the front cover of the book and invite the children to talk about the hijab worn by Asiya and describe it using adjectives.

- Explain to the children that they are going to design and describe a first-day hijab for Faizah to wear when she reaches the correct age. Give the children time to explore the different images of hijabs and fabrics available. Ask them to think about what sort of character Faizah is. Encourage the children to choose a design and colour for the hijab that they feel will reflect her personality. They should use the text to support their choices. Remind the children that Faizah said her first-day hijab would be 'blue too'. Ask them whether they think she would continue to think this or whether she might choose a different colour.

- When the children have created their designs, ask them to label their designs by writing descriptions on to sticky notes. Invite children to share their designs with the class.

3. Ordering events

Objective
To discuss the sequence of events in books and how items of information are related.

What you need
Copies of *The Proudest Blue*, slips of paper containing sentences from different parts of the story (one set for each child), large sheets of paper.

Cross-curricular link
Art

What to do

- Read *The Proudest Blue* as a class, taking it in turns to read sections using the 'jump in' strategy. (Start reading then say: *'x jump in'*. This child then reads until you choose the next child to jump in.)

- Give children individual copies of the text and encourage them to practise reading it with expression and fluency.

- Discuss the characters and settings in the story. Invite children to identify the order in which the characters and settings are introduced. Ask: *What do you think is the most important event in the story?* Tell them to share their ideas with a partner, then with another pair, then as a class.

- Give out the sentences on slips of paper. Tell the children to read and sequence the sentences according to when the events happened in the story. Bring the children back together and discuss the order of events, dealing with any sentences they were unsure about. Ask the children to stick the sentences in the correct order on a large sheet of paper and draw pictures to illustrate the main events. Invite children to take turns to read a sentence from their sequencing to retell the story as a class.

Differentiation

Support: Use decodable words within the children's phonic knowledge to rewrite short captions to tell the story. During the 'jump in' reading task, ensure children read a short section which is within their phonic skill-level.

Extension: Leave out some words from the sentences and encourage children to fill in the gaps using the correct word(s) from the text.

4. Creating characters

Objective
To draw on what they already know or on background information and vocabulary provided by the teacher.

What you need
Copies of *The Proudest Blue*, photocopiable page 20 'Creating characters' (two for each pair).

Cross-curricular link
PSHE

What to do

- Read *The Proudest Blue*. Tell the children to think about the characters in the story. Ask: *Who is the main character? Who is telling the story? Which character is older?* Encourage them to support their answers with evidence from the text.

- Display an enlarged copy of photocopiable page 20 'Creating characters'. Explain to the children that they are going to create character profiles of Asiya and Faizah in pairs. The outline of the person could be either character. Discuss the illustrations in the book and the colours used by the artist for the laughing, yelling boys. Tell the children to colour in the person on their sheet to show their feelings in the story. Ask: *Which colours would be suitable for Asiya? Which colours for Faizah?*

- Draw attention to the personalities of the characters that are developed through their actions, such as Faizah counting the number of steps across the playground.

- Model annotating the person by adding adjectives to describe their appearance and personality in the boxes. Begin by asking the children to use words from the word bank and then to think of other suitable adjectives of their own to describe Asiya and Faizah. Once the children have completed their character profiles, ask volunteers to share their profiles with the class.

Differentiation

Support: Children use the words provided in the word bank to annotate their characters. You may want to provide additional words.

Extension: Challenge children to write sentences containing their chosen adjectives using commas in a list.

5. Sparkling similes

Objective
To discuss word meanings, linking new meanings to those already known.

What you need
Copies of *The Proudest Blue*, a large sheet of blue fabric, small pieces of blue fabric, large pieces of paper.

Cross-curricular links
Art, PSHE

What to do
- Tell the children to sit on the carpet in a circle. Show them the large sheet of blue fabric. Encourage them to feel the fabric and, as a group, move it up and down in the air. With eyes closed, repeat the activity. Ask: *How does the fabric feel? How would you describe the colour of the fabric?* Use their ideas and descriptions to create a word bank on a large sheet of paper or a whiteboard.

- Encourage the children to think of as many different blue things as they can, taking turns to share ideas around the circle.

- Discuss the personification of the hijab in the story ('Her hijab smiles at me the whole way'; 'saying hello with a loud wave.') Ask: *Why do you think the author chose to use that vocabulary about the hijab? What was the purpose?* Share their ideas as a class.

- Choose some similes from the book and write them on a whiteboard or a large sheet of paper ('like the sky on a sunny day'; 'like the ocean waving to the sky'). Explain that similes are used by writers to create mental images for their readers and to make their texts more interesting. Discuss the use of the word 'like' to compare one item to another. As a class, create some examples of similes.

- Tell the children to stick small pieces of blue material onto a sheet of paper. Encourage them to add similes using the word bank created earlier and their additional ideas about the colour blue.

Differentiation
Support: Encourage children to generate their ideas orally.

Extension: Encourage children to use 'as... as a...' when comparing the blue material to another item.

6. Fantastic facts

Objective
To draw on what they already know or on background information and vocabulary provided by the teacher.

What you need
Copies of *The Proudest Blue*, copies of Extract 3, access to laptops or another form of IT, books about Islam, photocopiable page 21 'Fantastic facts'.

Cross-curricular link
RE

What to do
- Challenge the children to share with a partner as many facts as they can about the word 'hijab'. Set a time limit of five minutes. Remind them of previous activities, including the facts given in Extract 3.

- Explain that they are going to create a poster about Asiya, featuring three fantastic facts. Provide copies of Extract 3 to help the children recall facts. Model changing a fact from Extract 3 into a fact about Asiya. For example, 'Muslims believe in one God named Allah.' can be changed to 'Asiya is a Muslim who believes in one God named Allah.' Remind the children to use capital letters for proper nouns such as 'Muslim', 'Allah' and 'Asiya'.

- Ensure the children have access to information books or the internet in order to retrieve further information about Islam, what Asiya may have believed and what she might do in her daily life. Bring the children together at various points to allow them to share any interesting facts they have discovered.

- Once the children have decided on their three facts, tell them to write them within the outline on photocopiable page 21 'Fantastic facts' and colour the hijab bright blue. Ask volunteers to share their fantastic facts with the class and display the children's work.

Differentiation
Support: Children can work in small groups to generate one fact each to create a group poster about Asiya, using Extract 3 to help them.

Extension: Challenge children to use conjunctions within their facts to compare and contrast Asiya to themselves.

Creating characters

- Create a character profile of Asiya or Faizah.

- Write a different adjective in each box to describe their appearance and personality. Use the words below to help you.

Name:

nervous	beautiful	anxious
peaceful	strong	proud

Fantastic facts

- Create a poster about Asiya by colouring the hijab bright blue and adding your three fantastic facts about her.

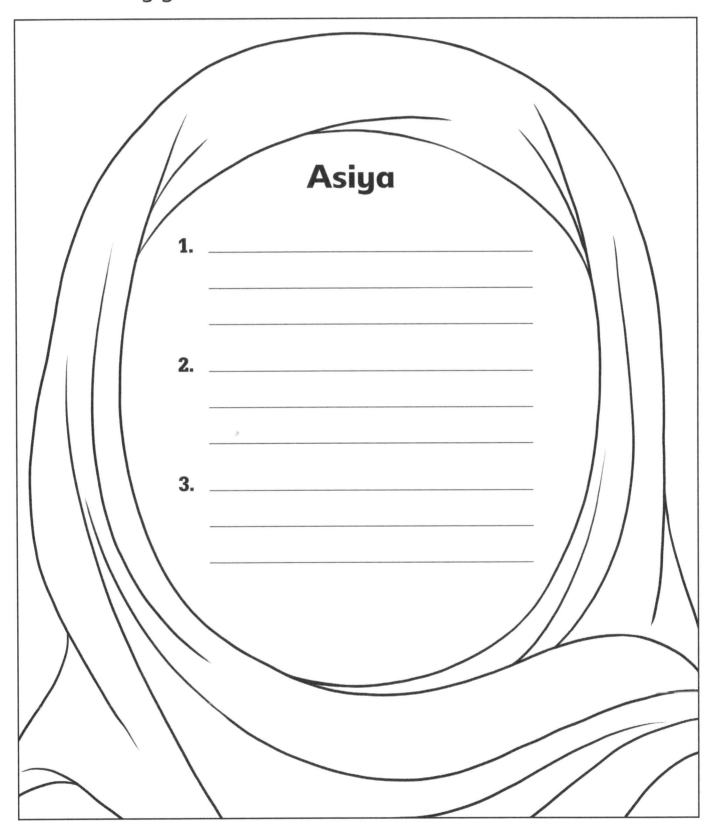

Asiya

1. _____

_____

_____

2. _____

_____

_____

3. _____

_____

TALK ABOUT IT ▶

1. How did you feel?

Objective
To articulate and justify answers, arguments and opinions.

What you need
Copies of *The Proudest Blue*

Cross-curricular links
PSHE, art

What to do
- Look through the book as a class, pausing on pages to discuss how the characters are feeling. Invite volunteers to share their thoughts and opinions. Look at the picture of Asiya heading into school wearing her first-day hijab. Ask: *How is Asiya feeling?* (carefree, happy, excited)

- Ask the children to think about the first time they did something new or a day in the future when they might do something for the first time. Invite them to talk in pairs about how they felt or might feel. Encourage them to use descriptive language and give reasons for their answers.

- Explain that they are going to draw a picture of themselves during that occasion. Encourage them to choose colours to reflect their feelings. Draw their attention to the colours used in the book at different points in the story.

- Challenge the children to add words describing their feelings around the picture (proud, nervous, sad, happy, apprehensive) and finish by inviting children to talk about their experiences using the vocabulary they have written.

Differentiation
Support: Encourage children to describe their feelings orally. Give them a forced alternative (for example, sad or happy) to choose if they cannot generate their own ideas.

Extension: Encourage children to use a variety of conjunctions within their oral sentences.

2. Dramatic dilemmas

Objective
To participate in role play and improvisations.

What you need
Copies of *The Proudest Blue*, scenarios from the text (including the characters involved) on cards.

Cross-curricular links
PSHE, drama

What to do
- Tell the children that they will be taking on the roles of characters from the story.

- Read aloud the advice given by Mama or display it. Ask the children to explain what was happening at that point in the story. Ask: *What do you think Mama means? Is it good advice?* Encourage the children to support their answers using examples from the story.

- Divide the class into three groups: the laughing/yelling boys, Asiya and Faizah. Invite a child to collect a card and read the scenario to the class. Ask the children to act out the scenario using actions, facial expressions and appropriate speech/sounds (for example, laughing).

- Challenge the group to whom the scene relates to explain how they might be feeling if they were that character. Invite children from the other groups to give advice on what they could do if they were in that situation. Discuss the advice and encourage others to evaluate it by agreeing with it or offering other suggestions.

- Repeat the activity using different scenario cards.

Differentiation
Support: Discuss the actions and speech required in a small group prior to children acting out the scenarios.

Extension: Encourage children to create their own direct speech as part of their role play.

3. Various vocals

Objective
To select and use appropriate registers for effective communication.

What you need
Prepared cards with different ways of using voice (for example, whispering, laughing, speaking like a giant, crescendo).

Cross-curricular link
Drama

What to do

- Tell the children to sit in a circle. Explain that they are going to be using their voices in different ways, including shouting, whispering and laughing, to read sections of the book. Some of these will reflect the way the characters felt during that part of the story.

- Begin by placing the cards in the centre of the circle and invite the children to each take a card. Read sections of the story, a sentence at a time, choosing children to read aloud. Their cards will determine how their sentence should be read out.

- Once a child has read aloud, ask: *Was that the correct way of speaking/reading that sentence?* Allow them to choose a more appropriate form of using their voice (for example, if they chose the 'like a giant' card for 'I don't know why a whisper came out.') Take turns saying the sentence in a different register until the children agree on the appropriate one.

- When all the cards have been used, divide the children into smaller groups. Give each group a different section of the text. Ask them to read their section, using an appropriate vocal register.

- Invite groups to share their readings. Encourage the other groups to offer feedback on use of register and suggest ways to make their communication more effective.

Differentiation

Support: Adults or peers model two ways of reading the section of text and children choose the appropriate one before echo reading it.

Extension: Encourage children to incorporate appropriate gestures and facial expressions when reading sections of the text.

4. How would you feel?

Objective
To participate in discussions and debates.

What you need
Photocopiable page 25 'How would you feel?' prepared into a set of cards for each group, small boxes, sticky notes.

Cross-curricular link
PSHE

What to do

- Explain to the children that they are going to work together to make a list of emotions felt by the characters in the book. Let them write or draw their ideas on sticky notes and add them to a working wall. Encourage them to recall why the character was feeling that way during that section of the book. Ask: *Did every character feel the same at that point? Why/why not?*

- In pairs, suggest that one partner chooses an emotion from the list created and the other guesses it from their partner's facial expression and actions. Bring the children together in a large circle and read through the list of emotions. Encourage the children to show appropriate facial expressions and gestures throughout. Invite children to add extra emotions to the list.

- Divide the class into smaller circles. In the centre of each circle, place the cards from photocopiable page 25 'How would you feel?' in a box. Tell the children to take turns to choose a card, read the question and answer it. Encourage the other children in the circle to discuss the response. Repeat the activity until all the cards have been chosen.

- As a whole class, share the outcomes of the group discussions. Begin by asking children to read aloud some of the questions. Encourage feedback by asking: *Which questions were challenging? Did anyone have conflicting ideas/emotions?*

Differentiation

Support: If possible, put children requiring emotional support into a circle where the discussion can be adult-led.

Extension: Encourage children to create additional scenarios to add to the cards.

5. Powerful performances

Objective
To give well-structured descriptions, explanations and narratives for different purposes, including for expressing feelings.

What you need
Copies of *The Proudest Blue*.

What to do

- Read *The Proudest Blue* as a class, using the echo reading technique. (The teacher reads a sentence, or section of the text, and asks the class to read it back in exactly the same way.) This activity is a good follow-up to 'Ordering events' (page 18) as the children will have practised sequencing the events in the story.

- Discuss the main events in the story and the reasons why they occurred. Show the children sections of the book in the wrong order and encourage them to talk about why the events could not have happened in this order (for example, Asiya getting her hijab after the boys were laughing).

- Organise the children into pairs. Using copies of the book, allow them time to practise retelling the story in their own words. Encourage them to use the pictures to support their oral storytelling and to take turns with their partner telling each part of the story.

- Bring the class together and invite the children to share feedback on their partner's retelling, using the sentence stem 'In my opinion…'. Encourage them to give ideas on how the retelling could be improved by altering their voice, adding information, expressing the feelings felt by the characters and explaining why events were happening. Encourage pairs to retell the story again, incorporating the suggestions given. Once all the children have participated in the retelling, give them time to discuss their performances.

Differentiation

Support: Place less confident learners in a pair/small group with supportive peers who they feel able to speak in front of.

Extension: Encourage more confident storytellers to take on the role of 'mentor', offering feedback and support to others.

6. True or false

Objective
To articulate and justify answers, arguments and opinions.

What you need
Prepared true/false cards with events from the story.

What to do

- As a class, read *The Proudest Blue* using choral reading techniques (the teacher and the children read the text together as a group). Pause at various points to ask questions about the events and how the characters are feeling. Ask: *Where are they going? How is Faizah feeling as she walks away from the yelling boy?*

- Recap the meanings of 'true' and 'false' by using examples from the classroom. Explain to the children that they will be asking and answering true or false questions about the story. Read a statement to the class: 'Asiya went to the beach wearing her first-day hijab.' Ask the children to discuss with a partner whether the statement is true or false. Encourage them to use the text to support their answer. (It is false because Asiya went to school wearing her first-day hijab.)

- Give pairs of children a set of statement cards. The children should take turns to read a statement from one of the cards with their partner answering it using 'true' or 'false' and the word 'because' to give reasons to support their answers. Encourage them to use examples from the book as justification.

- Allow time for the children to complete their discussions. Write two headings on the whiteboard: 'True' and 'False'. Invite children to stick their statements under the correct heading. Read through the statements in each column together and swap them if necessary.

Differentiation

Support: Allow children to use copies of the book to help them recall facts and identify whether statements are true or false.

Extension: Invite children to create their own true or false statements.

How would you feel?

Your friend laughs at you because you are wearing a new jacket. **How does this make you feel?**	A boy is shouting at one of your best friends because she doesn't like the same toys as him. **What would you say to him?**
Your best friend wins a competition for their drawing. **How does this make you feel? What would you do?**	Your favourite toy is lost. **How do you feel? What could your friends do to make you feel better?**
You and your friend both want to play with the same toy. **What could you do? If your friend took the toy, how would you feel?**	A girl in your class has a new pair of trainers. You don't like them. **What should you do?**
One of your friends is very shy. They sing a song in front of the whole school on their own. **How does this make you feel? What would you say to them?**	The girl you do not like in school says she loves your new bag. **How do you react? Why?**

GET WRITING ▶

1. Flowing formation

Objective
To write capital letters and digits of the correct size, orientation and relationship to one another and to lower-case letters.

What you need
Prepared capital letter and lower-case matching cards or magnetic letters, prepared sentences about the book including capital letters for names, individual whiteboards.

What to do
- Display the alphabet and sing an alphabet song with the children. Give out sets of lower-case letters or letter cards and invite the children to put them in alphabetical order. Encourage them to point to letters in response to letter names being said.

- Give each child a set of capital letters. Ask them to match the capital letters to the lower-case letters.

- Read through the alphabet using letter names then repeat using the sound each letter makes. Say a letter name or sound and ask the children to 'quick-write' the correct letter. Recap any letter formation that the children find difficult. (Children could be grouped according to their need; some may require individual support.)

- Once the formation activity has been completed, challenge the children to write sentences on their whiteboards about *The Proudest Blue*, using correct letter formation for both capital and lower-case letters. Bring the class together and invite volunteers to share their writing.

Differentiation
Support: Provide opportunities for children to form letters in various media, on vertical writing surfaces or to trace words.

Extension: Encourage children to use the diagonal and horizontal strokes needed to join letters.

2. Amazing adjectives

Objective
To use expanded noun phrases to describe and specify.

What you need
Copies of *The Proudest Blue*, cards with nouns from the story on ('backpack', 'street', 'hand', 'class', 'scarf', 'school').

What to do
- Write 'A princess' on the board. Ask the children to recall what type of word 'princess' is (a noun). Explain that they will be creating expanded noun phrases by adding adjectives to describe and specify the noun.

- Tell the children to write down as many adjectives as they can to describe a princess. Encourage them to describe her physical features and personality. Pick one suggestion from each description and add it to 'A princess' to make an expanded noun phrase ('A tall princess' or 'A grumpy princess').

- Introduce the noun cards. Invite the children to take a card from the pile and add an adjective to it to make it into an expanded noun phrase. Allow the children time to write expanded noun phrases for a selection of nouns from the story.

- Invite children to share their suggestions with the class. Ask: *Did anyone have the same adjectives? Which adjective is more powerful?*

- Read aloud a section of the book, adding the children's expanded noun phrases. Encourage them to consider whether the expanded noun phrase enhances the text or whether it alters the rhythm in a negative way.

Differentiation
Support: Provide adjective cards for children to choose from.

Extension: Encourage children to use a number of adjectives and commas in a list to create more complex expanded noun phrases.

3. Read all about it!

Objective
To develop positive attitudes towards and stamina for writing by writing for different purposes.

What you need
Copies of *The Proudest Blue*, newspapers and articles.

What to do

- Read *The Proudest Blue*, drawing the children's attention to the different events in the story and how the characters were feeling.

- Tell the children that they will be writing a newspaper report about Asiya's first day of wearing hijab to school. Use an example of a newspaper article to ensure that the children are aware of the structure and main features of a newspaper report (headline, facts about the main events, quotes and captions to accompany pictures).

- Look through the pictures in the book with the children. Invite volunteers to think of a good headline to accompany their article. Then ask the children, in pairs, to generate a caption. Discuss their suggestions as a class.

- Discuss the main events in the story and the order in which they occurred. Ask: *Which facts about the events do you think you need to include?*

- Choose a child to be Asiya and invite the rest of the class to ask questions about what happened and how she felt. Encourage them to collect ideas by taking notes.

- Allow the children time to draft their newspaper report. Remind them to re-read their ideas to check their meaning is clear. Bring the class together at various points to invite children to read sections of their report for feedback.

- Once children have re-read their writing, encourage them to write their report including the name of the newspaper, a headline, captions to accompany pictures and facts about the main event. (This could be done over a series of lessons.) Invite children to read their completed newspaper report to the class.

Differentiation
Support: Give children a word bank to support their spelling.

4. Suitable sequels

Objective
To plan or say out loud what they are going to write about.

What you need
Copies of *The Proudest Blue*, photocopiable page 29 'Suitable sequels'.

What to do

- Read *The Proudest Blue* with the children. Pose comprehension questions to ensure that the children know the main characters, events and how the characters are feeling throughout the story.

- Introduce the word 'sequel' and explain its meaning. Ask: *Can you think of any original stories or sequels that you have read?*

- Tell the children they are going to write their own sequel to *The Proudest Blue*, telling the story of what happens to Faizah when she can finally wear her first-day hijab. Stimulate ideas by asking: *What colour will her hijab be?* (remind children that she said it would be '*blue too*') *What will it remind her of? How will she feel? Will her experience be similar to Asiya's? Who else might be in the sequel?* Discuss possible titles for the sequel.

- Hand out photocopiable page 29 'Suitable sequels'. Read and discuss it together. The children should work in pairs and use the photocopiable page to share ideas and plan their writing. Revise the punctuation the children will need when writing their sequels and ensure that they understand the importance of sequencing ideas in narrative.

- Encourage the children to draft sections of their story to re-read, discuss with peers or an adult, and improve prior to writing their final version. Bring the class back together to read aloud their sequels. Discuss any similarities and differences between the original story and the sequel and between other children's sequels.

Differentiation
Support: Share ideas orally. Write as a group, focusing on punctuation, decoding using phonics and spelling common exception words.

Extension: Encourage children to compare Asiya's first-day hijab with Faizah's in their sequel.

5. Apology letters

Objective
To develop positive attitudes towards and stamina for writing by writing for different purposes.

What you need
Copies of *The Proudest Blue*, examples of letters.

Cross-curricular link
PSHE

What to do

- Display the sections of the book where the children are yelling and laughing at Asiya. Ask: *What is happening? Why?* Encourage the children to use the pictures and the information they already know to support their answers.

- Draw attention to the way the illustrator has portrayed the yelling/laughing children. Ask: *Why do you think they are a certain colour? Why don't they have faces?* Encourage the children to use examples from the story illustrations to support their answers.

- Discuss how the characters in the book feel during these events. Ask the children to think about the actions of the yelling/laughing boys and whether they made the right choice. Ask: *Do the yelling/laughing boys understand what Asiya is wearing? Why?*

- Talk about what the yelling/laughing boys should do next. (The boys' teacher may have explained what a hijab is and why Asiya is wearing one. Perhaps they could say sorry by writing a letter to Asiya.)

- Display an example letter and discuss its main features by highlighting and underlining them (sender's address, date, greeting, introduction, details, conclusion and ending). As a class, brainstorm ideas around the introduction, details and conclusion of a letter to Asiya from one of the yelling/laughing boys. Encourage the children to include the most important elements, such as saying sorry, and to give reasons for their actions and change in attitude.

- In small groups, ask the children to write a letter to Asiya from one of the boys apologising for his actions. Each group should appoint one child to be the scribe. Allow time for the groups to complete their letters and then share them with the class.

6. Dear Diary

Objective
To write narratives about personal experiences and those of others.

What you need
Copies of *The Proudest Blue*, examples of diary entries, photocopiable page 30 'Dear Diary'.

What to do

- Recap the main events from *The Proudest Blue*. Invite children to say how Asiya is feeling during each event and why. Encourage them to use examples from the text and illustrations to support their answers.

- Tell the children that they are going to write a diary entry about Asiya's first day wearing hijab to school. Display an example diary entry and hand out copies to the class. Talk the children through the different criteria by highlighting and underlining sections of the diary text (date/time, past tense, use of first person 'I', 'my', 'we', 'our', events in the correct order, feelings, time-linking words 'next', 'first', 'then', where it happened). Ask the children to find and highlight the different criteria on their own copy.

- Hand out photocopiable page 30 'Dear Diary' and allow the children time to write down their ideas in note form. Once they have the notes, they should write a draft version of the diary. As a class, decide on a date/time together. Use the book illustrations to help inform the time of year.

- Bring the children together and ask them to share a couple of sentences orally from their drafts. Encourage constructive feedback. Using their draft ideas, children should then write their diary entry from Asiya's point of view. Once completed, invite the children to share their diary entries. Ask the other children to check they have included each of the diary-writing criteria from the checklist.

Differentiation

Support: Supply children with a word bank and template to fill in to help them write their diary entries.

Extension: Encourage children to use different types of sentences rather than only using statements.

Suitable sequels

● Fill in this table to help you plan your own sequel to
The Proudest Blue.

Main character	Other characters

Faizah's hijab	
Adjectives	Similes

Beginning	Feelings
Opener...	
Middle	Feelings
End	Feelings

Dear Diary

● Plan your diary entry about Asiya's first day wearing hijab to school.

Criteria	Notes	Included in my draft? ✔/✗
Date/time		
Past tense		
Use of first person		
Events in order		
Feelings		
Time-linking words		
Where it happened		

ASSESSMENT ▶

1. Delightful dictation

Objective
To write from memory simple sentences dictated by the teacher that include words using the GPCs, common exception words and punctuation taught so far.

What you need
Four prepared sentences for dictation that meet the above objective (could include questions, exclamations and statements), individual whiteboards.

What to do

- Explain to the children that they are going to write some sentences to see how well they can spell words and use punctuation. Revise the punctuation that the children have learned so far, including capital letters, full stops, exclamation marks and question marks. You could use examples from *The Proudest Blue* when recapping this.

- Tell the children that you will read aloud a sentence while they listen. (Ensure the sentences increase in complexity in order to assess each child.) Remind the children how important it is to spell the words correctly and to use the correct punctuation. They should use their knowledge of phonics and common exception words to spell words correctly.

- Read each sentence slowly to the children. Allow them time to write it down on a whiteboard and re-read it to check it makes sense and they have punctuated it correctly.

- Take photos of the children's work, then write the sentences on the board for children to self-correct. Discuss any misconceptions and incorrect punctuation.

Differentiation

Support: Provide some simple captions at phase 2 phonics level.

Extension: Ensure a variety of sentence types and exception words are included.

2. What do you know?

Objective
To understand books by answering and asking questions.

What you need
Copies of *The Proudest Blue*, a worksheet containing ten questions about the text (including how, what, where, when, who, why), coloured pens for marking.

What to do

- Explain to the children that they will be demonstrating what they know about *The Proudest Blue*. Allow time for them to scan the text to refresh their comprehension. Encourage them to ask questions to ensure they understand the text.

- Work as a class on some sample questions, modelling how to answer them using retrieval techniques and using the text and illustrations to support answers. Include each question type during this part of the lesson.

- Give out the worksheet and copies of *The Proudest Blue*. Challenge the children to answer the questions by writing in sentences and using the text to support their answers. Remind the children that words which occur in the text should be spelled correctly.

- Once the children have completed the questions, they should swap their answers with a partner. Supply each child with a coloured pen (in line with the school's marking policy). Read through the questions and invite children to share their answers. The children should peer mark their partner's work. For incorrect answers, encourage partners to give constructive feedback.

Differentiation

Support: Supply children with multiple choice answers or complete the questions orally with an adult.

Extension: Children to complete 'why' questions and to model proving their answers to the class.

3. Clever contractions

Objective

To learn to spell more words with contracted forms.

What you need

Individual whiteboards, a worksheet containing sentences with the long form of words to be contracted. (You may wish to use sentences from *The Proudest Blue*. For example, 'I do not know why a whisper came out.' 'It's the most beautiful first day of school ever.')

What to do

- Tell the children that they are going to learn to spell more words with contracted forms. Remind them about the reading activity that they have already completed ('The long and short of it', page 16). Invite volunteers to explain the meaning of 'contracted form'.

- Model writing a word containing an apostrophe on the board and emphasise where it is situated (towards the top of the tall letters, rather than on the line like a comma). Say a long form of the word, for example, 'do not'. Tell the children to write it on their whiteboard. Now ask children to write down the contracted form of the word.

- When they have finished, ask them to swap boards with their partner. Write the correct contracted form on the board. Ask partners to assess whether the contracted form of the word is spelled correctly. Repeat the activity with different words.

- Write on the board a sentence with the contracted form of a word missing. ('Some people _____ understand your hijab.') Invite a child to write the missing word ('won't') in the space. Ask the rest of the class to read the sentence and say whether the word is correct and has been spelled correctly.

- Hand out the prepared sheet of sentences containing the long form of words. Allow time for the children to complete the sentences by adding the contracted forms, then bring the class together to share their words and spellings.

Differentiation

Support: Supply a word bank of contracted words for children to choose from.

4. Perfect punctuation

Objective

To use sentences with different forms: statement, question, exclamation, command.

What you need

Copies of *The Proudest Blue*, prepared statements, exclamations, commands and questions from *The Proudest Blue* without punctuation.

What to do

- Display on the board an example of a statement, an exclamation, a command and a question. Explain to the children that there are four sentence types on the board (statement, command, exclamation and question). Allow time for the children to read them. For each sentence, ask: *Which type of sentence is this? How do you know?*

- Show the children a different example of the four sentence types with the punctuation removed. Challenge them to explain which is which now.

- Remind the children of the rules for each type of sentence. (Statements are sentences that tell you something. They usually end with a full stop. Questions are sentences that ask you something. They usually end with a question mark. Commands are sentences that tell you to do something. They are found in instructions but can also be quite short and angry. They can end with a full stop or an exclamation mark. An exclamation is a sentence beginning with 'what' or 'how'. It is a full sentence, including a verb, which ends with an exclamation mark.)

- Provide the children with some prepared sentences from the text, without punctuation. Challenge them to sort the sentences into the four types. Once complete, ask the children to correctly punctuate each one using capital letters, full stops, exclamation marks or question marks. Invite volunteers to read their sentences with appropriate expression.

Differentiation

Support: Ask children to sort statements and questions into the correct category and add the correct punctuation (full stop or question mark).

Extension: Invite children to create their own examples of the sentence types including the correct punctuation.